Angela Fannin

Jerry Fannin

The Armadillo
Handbook

The Complete
Unabridged

ARMADILLO
HANDBOOK

All you wanted to know about Armadillos and were afraid to ask

Photographs and
Cartoons by
Jerry W. Fannin

Text by
Angela Farris Fannin

Acknowledgments

We would like to express our appreciation to the following people for their assistance in the preparation of this book:

Sharri Shaw, Noah C. Cole, Mark Homeyer, Joey Jones, Effie R. Hibbetts, Michael Fowler, John Paul Jones, Bennett Macik, Steven Homeyer, Barbara Jones, Buddy Fannin, Bob Graham, Jeff Farris, Jr., Herman Homeyer Jr., Karen Jones, Cecilia Marek, Larry Andrews, Clare Bass, and J.D. Robertson.

FIRST EDITION

FIRST PRINTING

Copyright © 1982
By Jerry and Angela Fannin

Published in the United States of America
By Eakin Press, P.O. Drawer AG, Burnet, Texas, 78611

ISBN 0-89015-325-6

ABOUT THE AUTHOR

A love of Texas lore and life inspired native Texan Jerry W. Fannin to create the photographs and cartoons for *The Complete Unabridged Armadillo Handbook.* His wife, Angela, composed the text. Both are graduates of Sam Houston University. They are the parents of a son, Blair, who made the accompanying photo. Their previous creative work includes the popular novelty book, *Johnnies, Biffies, Outhouses, Etc.,* which immortalizes the outdoor toilet in words and pictures. Enthusiasm for the armadillo as a part of Texas lore led to the publication of *The Complete Unabridged Armadillo Handbook* which provides a permanent record of everything you've always wanted to know about the armadillo.

Photo by Blair L. Fannin

ARMADILLO
(Dasypus novemcinctus)

Introduction

Armadillo time in Texas is any day in the cool of evening when those nine-banded little creatures come from their burrow to dine on insects such as termites and ants. In the early days of Texas the armadillo was found only in areas near the border of Mexico. Their habitat now includes most of Texas as well as Mississippi, Alabama, Georgia, Florida, and parts of South Carolina.

Because the armadillo does not thrive in captivity, it is difficult to study under controlled observation. The mysterious quality of its personality as well as its unusual appearance contributes to its current popularity among Texans and non-Texans alike.

The current "armadillo-mania" led to an appeal by a group of school children who petitioned the state legislature to name the armadillo the official state mammal of Texas. Even though the request was denied, Texans in business enterprises of many kinds have chosen the armadillo as their trademark.

The number of armadillos in any area of Texas depends on the existence of predators. Two natural predators of the armadillo, the coyote and the wolf, are rapidly becoming extinct. The armadillo favors areas featuring a loose soil that can be moved easily.

Eradicating the armadillo may be accomplished by gun, trap, or both. The armadillo trap is a corridor shaped device made of wire. Once the armadillo ambles inside, the door automatically closes and makes retreat impossible. The trap is an aid to the home gardener annoyed by the armadillo's digging in vegetable gardens and flower beds.

Another killer of this creature is the automobile. The armadillo's automatic fright response makes it impossible for him to escape a rapidly moving car. The slow-witted and slow-moving creature spontaneously jumps into the air.

After the death of the animal has been accomplished, there are many uses for the meat and shell. The meat can be barbecued or stewed while the shell can be made into baskets and lampshades.

Even though the animal moves slowly, it is a participant in popular competitive races. The armadillo race occurs in parts of Texas where the animal is prolific. New Braunfels is the site of an annual armadillo competition. A chili cook-off accompanies the race.

In spite of the armadillo's strangeness or maybe because of it, Texans delight in presenting the armadillo as an unofficial mascot of our state. As long as there are armadillos people will continue to enjoy this elusive little creature who was first discovered and named by the Spaniards of early Texas.

TEXAS TURKEY

A scaled, hard-covered creature gave Texas 'lore its charm
A nine-banded enigma causing little harm

The Spaniards called the creature, "Little Armored One"
While later generations coined "Texas Turkey,"
"Hoover Hog," and "Texas Submarine"

Texans use them in chili and race them for fun
While school children rant for a state mammal — just one!

The "Aggadillo" abounds in Aggieland
While Armadillo-Mania spreads with every man

Immortalized on T-Shirts, pencils, and caps
Emblazoned on glasses, pillows, and maps

A lover of insects who swims and plays dead
Yet gives birth to 4, all either boy or girl

The "diller" we love, we'll honor him o'er and o'er
He's a part of Texas we Texans adore.

Angela Farris Fannin

The Legend of the Texas Armadillo

Long ago Indians roamed the plains and hills of Texas. The land belonged to the Coahuiltecans, Karankawas, Tonkawas, Comanches, Apaches, Caddos, and others. The land and buffalo was theirs. The freedom and beauty of nature belonged to the Indian.

Soon, men of other nations came to claim the land called Texas. At the time of the white man's invasion a Coahuiltecan warrior reposing under a mesquite tree had a dream. A voice told him that soon the Indians would be overpowered and eradicated by the white man. Orders were given to approach each Texas Indian tribe for the purpose of stealing an animal for sacrifice. The sacrificial offering was to counteract the destruction of the Indians in Texas. The warrior arose from the dream and began the journey to each tribe.

He approached the outskirts of the Caddo nation in the "piney woods" with extreme caution. Wild hogs were plentiful in the heavily guarded region dominated by the Caddo. Almost as strange as the dream itself, there was a sudden appearance of a wild hog bound tightly to a tall pine tree. As the warrior began to release the hog, he was attacked by a band of Caddo braves. To his astonishment he began to speak the Caddo tongue. The warrior told of his mission and of his need

for the wild hog. The Caddo braves released him and sent him on his way.

The fierce Karankawas of huge physical proportions greeted the warrior with well-sharpened knives and spears. Again, he lapsed into the native tongue of the tribe and requested a turtle for the fulfillment of his mission. They tied the sea creature to the rope with the wild hog.

As he approached each tribe, the same succession of events occurred. He lapsed into the native tongue of the opposing tribe while the spell made them docile providers. The Apaches supplied a buffalo while the Comanches provided a horse. The Tonkawas added a turkey; the Wichitas, a snake; the Jumanos, a bird; and the Atakapans, a deer. His own tribe, the Coahuiltecans, provided a fish.

After collecting the assortment of animals, he was overcome by a deep sleep. On awakening he viewed the ground around him with amazement. The spot once occupied by the wild hog showed only a trickle of a thick, black substance. The area formerly occupied by the turtle gurgled with a clear spring water of coolness and freshness unsurpassed by Texas streams. The buffalo chips were gone. Fragments of a shiny, yellow substance remained instead. Remnants of the horse took the form of hard, black particles which ignited under proper conditions. The area occupied by the turkey produced a wealth of gaseous fumes exuding from the earth. A small tree with long needles sprouted where

the snake once rested. In place of the bird, there was succulent fruit that was new and strange to the palate of the warrior. The deer had been replaced by an even larger four-legged creature with horns of unusual length and diameter. Finally, the warrior's own fish had disappeared. In its place he found a few small, round objects of a white pearlescent beauty — gifts from the sea.

The Coahuiltecan warrior became enraged. With fierce emotion and great display of strength, he gathered the remnants of the animal menagerie into a mound. Feeling that the spirit from above had betrayed him, he stalked back to the tribal camp.

As the invading Spaniards passed the spot, they noticed the mound penetrated by a single hole. From the hole emerged a strange creature encased in a hard shell-like covering. After a close examination they discovered the creature had nine bands of indestructible armor. They called it, "armadillo," which means "little armored one."

The nine-banded armadillo remains as an offering from the tribes of Indians who once roamed the hills and plains of Texas and discovered the great natural resources of the state.

"Armadillo Den"

True Facts About The Texas Armadillo

The name was given to the hard-shelled animal by the Spaniards of early Texas. It means "little armored one."

The nine-banded armadillo is found only in North America. The area near the Mexican border was occupied by the first Texas armadillos. Their range now includes Mississippi, Alabama, Georgia, Florida, and parts of South Carolina.

The diet of the armadillo includes insects, earthworms, spiders, land snails, ants, fire ants, and termites. Studies of the food habits of the mammal show that 488 different items are eaten.

Small teeth in the back of the mouth prevent the armadillo from biting their attacker.

The band of small, bony, jointed plates across the back of the armadillo permits the nine-banded variety to curl into a ball as a protective measure against the enemy. Sparse projections of fine, wispy hair are visible on the shell.

The burrow or den of the armadillo is made by the fierce digging of its strong claws into soft soil. It is an excellent trap for insects. The armadillo may build the den exclusively for this purpose.

"Sniffing"

The den of the armadillo may be 2 to 15 feet in length and 4 feet in depth. When the burrow is used for breeding, the armadillo makes a large nest of leaves, grasses, and plants.

Breeding time for the armadillo is between June and September. After copulation, the embryo remains suspended until conditions are appropriate for gestation and birth. Culmination of the pregnancy occurs in the spring when food is plentiful.

The male armadillo selects a mate from two or three females. Breeding occurs when the female is two years old.

A litter consists of four babies that are of the same sex who feed on milk from the mother. Baby armadillos are rarely seen since they spend the first six months of life underground.

The armadillo meat is delicious when prepared properly.

Since they are a nervous mammal, the armadillo race may cause death from shock.

Regions containing movable soil boast a larger number of armadillos per acre. Walker County has very sandy soil which permits a ratio of one armadillo for every three acres of land.

The spontaneous fright reaction of the armadillo is to jump into the air. This explains the appearance of many dead ones on the highways.

The armadillo is sensitive to extreme cool or hot weather. In the heat of summer they are active in the cool of the evening while cold winter days drive them out of their burrows in mid-afternoon. Long periods of freezing weather eliminate the armadillo.

Scientists are using armadillos in research designed to develop a vaccine against leprosy.

The armadillo has the ability to consume excessive amounts of air causing the stomach to swell. In direct contrast the gravity of the animal allows him to sink to the bottom of a stream or river in order to walk on the bottom. The stomach inflates when air is needed which permits him to come to the surface.

A caged armadillo lives for a short time due to rapid dehydration produced by frequent urination. They must be given large amounts of water. As a general rule, the armadillo is not a suitable pet.

The armadillo may roll on his back and play dead. This is "fainting" caused by the primitive nervous system of the animal.

The animal has extremely poor vision in the daytime but has a sensitivity to the smell of his surroundings.

The strong scent surrounding the armadillo comes from special glands near the posterior of the body. The odor increases when the animal becomes excited. Butchering the armadillo for cooking removes any desire for eating the meat.

Senator Jack Ogg proclaimed the armadillo mascot of the State of Texas. His supporters included students of the Oak Creek Elementary School, Spring Texas: (L to R) Donna Snow, Jane Allen, Senator Jack Ogg (Back to front) Greg Lado, Sloan Childers, and Clark Childers.

Courtesy of Katherine Staat, Senate Media Services

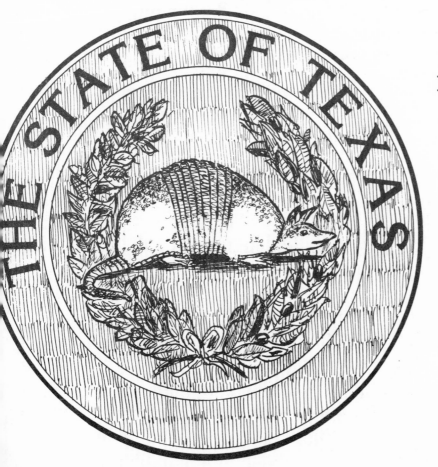

The Armadillo
National Mammal of Texas

★

Representatives of the children of Oak Creek Elementray School in the Spring Independent School District appeared before the state legislature with a request to name the armadillo the official state mammal of Texas. Their efforts were rewarded by a proclomation issued by Senator Jack Ogg during his reign as governor-for-a-day on October 3, 1981. The proclomation elevated the armadillo to the status of recognized mascot of the state of Texas.

PROCLAMATION
GOVERNOR JACK OGG
OCTOBER 3, 1981

WHEREAS, The great State of Texas is known for its unique symbols, including longhorns, oil wells, cowboys and cactus; and

WHEREAS, It is now appropriate that we now recognize the armadillo as a symbol of Texas; and

WHEREAS, This resolution has been prepared by the students of Oak Creek Elementary School in Harris County representing the students and children of Texas who all agree that the nine-banded armadillo, whose skin is as tough as a cowboy's boot; and

WHEREAS, The armadillo is a hardy, pioneering creature that chose to begin migrating here about the time Texas became a state; and

WHEREAS, The armadillo possesses many remarkable and unique traits, some of which parallel the attributes that distinguish a true Texan, such as a deep respect and need for the land, the ability to change and adapt, and a fierce, undying love for freedom; and

WHEREAS, The students of Oak Creek Elementary School found a fact of interest representing each band of the armadillo as follows:

1. Like many residents of the great State of Texas, the armadillo prefers the days of sunshine and warmth to those of freezing temperatures;

2. The armadillo's sense of smell can warn him of danger or lead him to lunch as quickly as a Texan can sniff out a barbecue or a chilli cook-off;

3. The hide and armor of the armadillo make him tough and unafraid of brambles, thorns, and tough terrain;

4. When startled, the armadillo can move as fast as a running back from the Oilers or the Cowboys (his fine reputation as a racer is well known);

5. The armadillo is an excellent burrow builder, and just as Texans provide homes for refugees from northern states, the armadillo generously vacates his burrow so that other creatures may have shelter;

6. Unperturbed by water, the armadillo can walk on a creek bed under the water or float across the creek, whichever he chooses to be appropriate;

7. Proving his usefulness to man, the armadillo, as a research animal, holds the key to the cure of leprosy, and he also labors to rescue Texas from the fire ant by eating every one he finds;

8. Carrying on the fine tradition of Texans as goodwill ambassadors around the world, four West Texas armadillos have recently set up housekeeping in the Peking, China zoo;

9. And, finally, the armadillo reflects the good humor of the residents of Texas who proudly display his likeness on T-shirts, belt buckles, and pickup truck windows; now,

THEREFORE, be it known, that I, JACK OGG, as Governor of the State of Texas, do hereby proclaim the Nine-Banded armadillo, daspus novemcinctus mexicanus, a recognized mascot of the State of Texas.

In testimony whereof, I have hereunto signed my name and caused the Seal of the State to be affixed at the City of Austin, this the 3rd day of October A.D., 1981.

Attest:

SECRETARY OF STATE

GOVERNOR OF TEXAS

Courtesy of Senator Jack Ogg and Larry McGinnis

G. W. Strake, Jr.

Jack Ogg

What To Feed An Armadillo

- Scarab Beetles
- Termites
- Ants
- Caterpillars
- Earthworms
- Crayfish
- Birds' Eggs
- Tomatoes
- Melons
- Berries
- Fungi
- Carrion
- Maggots

Reflections . . . About Armadillos

"The first armadillo I ever saw was about 1915. I thought it was a snake when I saw the tail. We carried it to the house and my Daddy knew what it was. The negroes on the home place said it was a 'grave digger.' White folks and negroes wouldn't come out of the house at night for a week. They were scared of them back then."

Contributed by a true Texian

(the real way to spell Texan)

"One day Daddy and I were going to town in the wagon. Mammy Tobe met us out by the road and asked us if we'd ever seen an armadillo. She had it in a box. I was about five years old (that was about 1914) and that was the first armadillo that I'd ever seen.

Contributed by a Madison County Citizen

★ ★ ★

"The hardest fall I ever got in my life was caused by an armadillo. My horse was loping along Wixon Creek when he stepped in an armadillo hole and threw me into a haystack."

Contributed by a Brazos County Citizen

★ ★ ★

"Up at Kosse, you know we grew up at Kosse. Well, my granddaddy had a bunch of willow trees. He dug up the willows and left holes filled with roots. Old Taso, our dog, sniffed out armadillos in those holes and gnawed at 'em until his teeth wore down to the gums and bled. That's a fact.

Contributed by a Yarn Spinner

★ ★ ★

"I cooked a 'diller one time. Every time I took a bite I could hear it moan, "Ugh!" I've never had a taste for 'diller meat since."

Contributed by a Well Digger

"I figured out how to get an armadillo out of his hole. Catch ahold of his tail and wait until he stops pullin' then give him a yank and he'll come right out."

Contributed by Effiediller

"I was workin' on the railroad at Lometa, Texas, in the 1940s. I glanced up a hill and there were some piggy lookin' things rootin' up the ground. I asked some people if those were a new breed of hawgs. They laughed and said, "Ain't you ever seen a 'diller?""

Contributed by a New Mexico Traveler

"Root Marks"

"Armadillo Tracks"

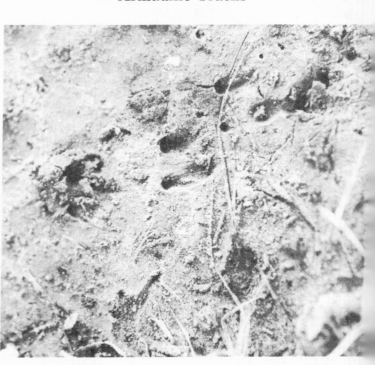

"Snout"

"Claws"

"Ears"

POPULAR LOCATIONS OF

THE NINE BANDED

ARMADILLO IN TEXAS

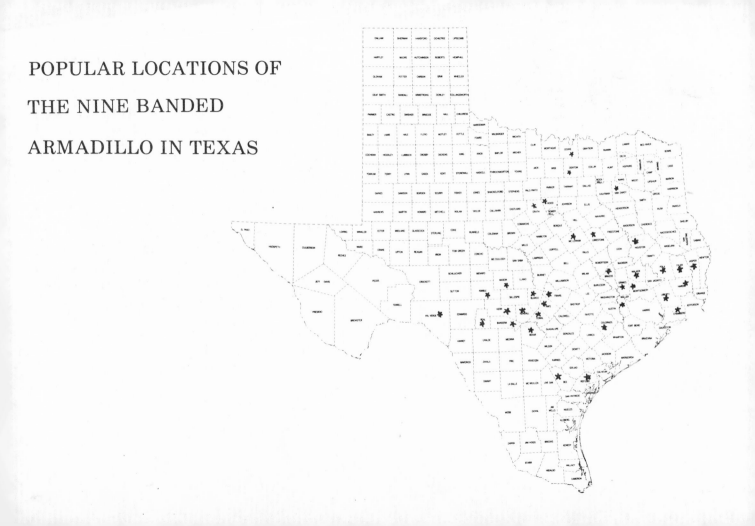

"Armadillo Tall Tales"

"Limestone County, Texas"

"When I lived over in Limestone County we went 'diller huntin' one night. 'Hit was just about sundown an' thar' was varmits everwhar'. I never seen so many 'dillers in mah life.

Wal, I had a ol' speckled pup that hadn't never been out lookin' fer 'dillers. Th' other dawgs, they took off an' smelled up one real quick-like. But Jasper (that was mah pup) he rared back an' froze. Them 'dillers jus' skeered him half ta death.

'Bout that time a 'diller jumped right on top 'a that dawg an' he fell over dead, right thar — of fright! Darndest thang I ever seen. 'Course that wuz when I lived over in Limestone County."

Contributed by East Texas Sam

"Grandma's 'Diller Den"

"Mah Grandma come from Arkansas. She said she never saw no 'dillers 'til she got ta Texas. Wal, one day her garden was plumb dug up by 'dillers. Ever' day 'hit was th' same ol' thang. Them 'dillers jes' ruint th' 'taters.

That night she wuz ready. She tied up some rocks in one of mah old nightgowns. That wuz a real good weepon. Wal, she said she never seen nothin' like it. Thar' wuz about 25 'dillers that just come out all at once an' they wuz rootin' an' snortin' like nothin' you ever seen. Now this wuz in th' ol' days.

Wal, Grandma commenced ta fallerin' them 'dillers. When she come ta th' 'diller den she had her slang ready. 'Bout that time she saw a giant 'diller come out of a hol' in th' groun' an' Grandma begin ta run. She said they always called that neck of th' woods, th' 'diller den an' she never went back thar' agin'."

Contributed by 'Diller Annie

"Poor Man's Hawg"

"That wuz a hard year, 1929. We wuz despert' for sumthin' ta eat. We had them bread lines, but ah don' tak' nothin' from nobody. Ah said, wal, we'll jes' eat 'diller.

Ah set out with mah gun an' ole Blue, mah dawg. We wuz jes' comin' ta Cut'N Shoot, Texas, when ah saw a whole herd of 'dillers rootin' 'round a big pine tree.

Ah took aim an' them 'dillers begin ta charge at me an' ah begin ta far'. 'Bout six or seven fell daid 'an ah set out ta home with 'em in a sack. Halfway there ah met a city feller what wuz fell on good times. He wuz dressed fit ta kill. He saw them 'dillers hangin' out of mah sack an' ast' me what they wuz. Ah tol' him they wuz hawgs an' he wuz welcom' to 'em for a price. Wal, he giv' me money fer them 'dillers an' set out ta home with them poor man's hawgs."

Contributed by Depression's Child

"Snipe Huntin"

One night we wuz huntin' snipes in Jasper County. Now, if ya' ain't never been snipe huntin' then ya' really missed somethin'. Wal, we got uh toe sack an' held it open for 'em snipes. Cuzin' Joe Dan let out the call and waited. About that time a giant 'diller cum out of uh brush pile. He had the biggest ears ah ever seen. His ears wuz so big they poked thru' th' sack. Joe Dan's cowboy boots wuz so big they crushed th' tips of 'em big 'diller's ears. 'At's why 'dillers has short ears!

Contributed by a Coon Hunter

"Gravediggers"

"Mah Mammy tol' me 'bout this when she liv' down at Phelps, Texas, befo' she wuz free. Walka' County is jes' ful' of awmadillas. Thea's mo' 'dillas in that place than you can shake a stick at.

Untie Lizzie wuz buried on a hill under some pine trees away from th' house. About fo' weeks afta' she passed on Mammy stopped ta check on th' grave. 'Dillas wuz diggin' up th' place an' eatin' on Untie Lizzie. We calls 'em 'dillas gravediggers."

Contributed by a descendant of a slave

Armadillo Baskets

Manufacture of baskets, lampshades, and other souvenir items made from the armadillo was once the basis for a large local industry in Texas. The trade flourished near the border of Mexico. The popularity of lampshades and baskets made from the shell of the armadillo has declined since World War I. The following tips are helpful for the beginning craftsman who wants to make an armadillo basket.

1. Remove the flesh and entrails of the animal.
2. Degrease the outer and inner surfaces of the shell by using a mixture of water and detergent.

3. Apply a dry, powdered preservative to the inside of the shell.
4. Inject a liquid preservative such as formaldehyde into the head area.
5. Bend the tail toward the head forming a handle for the basket. (Anchor firmly.)
6. Place crushed newspaper inside the cavity until the shell dries to the desired shape. Pack the newspaper tightly. Secure the exterior shape by wrapping with string.
7. Spray the exterior of the shell with lacquer.
8. Line the interior of the shell with fabric. Attach with glue.

Let's Eat Armadillo!

The rural folks of East Texas have known of the delicious meat of the armadillo for years. When cooked properly, it resembles pork.

The cook should select a young armadillo for tenderness. The armadillo must be cleaned by splitting the animal underneath and removing the entrails. The meat is extracted from the shell then cooked in a pit. Pit cookery requires 24 hours. An alternative quick method of cookery is frying the armadillo like chicken.

Directions for Preparing The Pit

1. Dig a hole that will accommodate the size of the armadillo.
2. Line the hole with foil or large leaves.
3. Cover the hole with a metal sheet of iron or tin.
4. Place hot coals over the lid.

Place the armadillo in the pit after marinating it in the following mixture.

Marinade for Pit Cooked Armadillo

2 sticks margarine
3 level Tablespoons of cornstarch
1 bottle of Worcestershire sauce
1 cup cold water

Melt margarine. Dissolve cornstarch in water and add to Worcestershire sauce. Stir in melted margarine. Marinate armadillo in mixture overnight then brush with the remaining liquid as it cooks.

Sauce (To be served with cooked armadillo meat)

1 Tablespoon chili powder (or to taste)
½ teaspoon garlic powder
½ cup onion, chopped
2 Tablespoons salad oil
2 Tablespoons red wine vinegar
¼ cup brown sugar
¼ cup lemon juice
Salt and pepper to taste
1 cup catsup
½ cup water

Simmer for 15 minutes. Serve over armadillo meat cooked in pit.

Poor Man's Armadillo Stew

Meat from one young armadillo; cut into cubes; salt and pepper to taste.

Dredge meat in flour; brown in 2 Tablespoons of cooking oil in large skillet.

In separate utensil in small amount of oil brown:
½ cup chopped onion
¼ cup chopped celery

Add the above to the meat with:
1 large can stewed tomatoes
2 Tablespoons chili powder
¼ teaspoon garlic powder
1 large potato (pared and cubed)

Simmer for one hour or until ingredients are tender. Add water as needed to give desired thickness to stew.

Serve in large bowls with corn chips, crackers, or garlic bread.

Armadillo Chili

2 cans of tomatoes (16 oz.-purée in blender)
1 can of tomato paste (8 oz.)
2 cups of chopped onion
2 cups of chopped green pepper
2 minced cloves garlic
2 Tablespoons of salad oil
¼ cup minced parsley
3 pounds of ground armadillo meat (made from 3 medium size armadillos or 2 large armadillos)
⅓ cup chili powder (to taste)
1 Tablespoon salt
1 teaspoon pepper
Water as needed

Sauté onion and green pepper in oil. Brown meat in separate skillet. Add green pepper, onions, tomatoes, and tomato paste to meat mixture. Add remaining seasonings and simmer 1½ hours or until meat is tender. Cooked pinto beans may be added. Serve with crackers or corn chips.

Ginger-Dillos

1   cup margarine
1   cup brown sugar
1   egg
1   cup molasses
2   Tablespoons vinegar
5   cups all-purpose flour
1½ teaspoons soda
½   teaspoon salt
1   Tablespoon ginger
1   teaspoon cinnamon
1   teaspoon ground cloves

Cream margarine with sugar and add egg, molasses and vinegar. Beat well. Sift dry ingredients together and stir in. Chill at least three hours. Roll thin on lightly floured surface. Cut with armadillo-shaped cookie cutter, sprinkle with granulated sugar and bake 6 to 8 minutes on lightly-greased sheet at 375 degrees. Makes 12 dozen tasty Ginger-Dillos!

Recipe by Carole H. Allen
Creator of the Texas
Good Luck Baking Kit

BIBLIOGRAPHY

Bode, Dale. Naturalist, Brazos Valley Museum of Natural History, "Midday in the Brazos Valley" (Television Interview). August, 1981.

Davis, William B. *The Mammals of Texas*. Bulletin No. 41, Texas Parks and Wildlife Service, Revised 1978. 294 pp.

Kalmbach, Edwin Richad. *The Armadillo*. Fish and Wildlife Service, 1943. 61 pp.

Morehead, Judith and Richard. *The Texas Wild Game Cookbook*. Encino Press: Austin, 1972. 81 pp.

Newcomb, W.W. Jr. *The Indians of Texas*. University of Texas Press: Austin, 1961. 404 pp.

"Outdoors South, September," *Southern Living*, Vol. 16, No. 9:40-44, September 1981.

Palermo, Mike, Taxidermist, Palermo Taxidermy Shop, Bryan, Texas. Telephone Interview, September 24, 1981.

Ramsey, Charles. "Fact Sheet, Armadillo," Texas Agricultural Extension Service, The Texas A&M University System: L-1663.

Sweeten, Mary K. "Small Game." Texas Agricultural Extension Service, The Texas A&M University System: MP-1345.

The Houston Chronicle, August 3, 1981. Section 6, p. 8, "Science Turns to Armadillos in Research to Fight Leprosy."

The World Book Encyclopedia, I, p. 679. Chicago: Worldbook-Childcraft International, 1979.

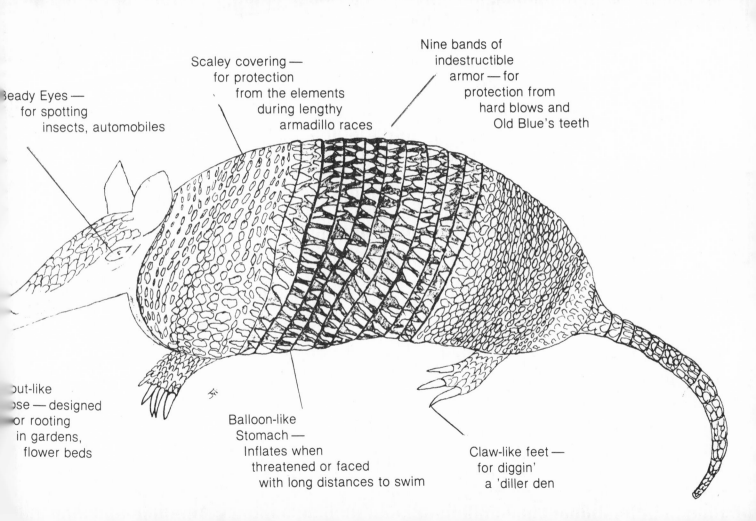

Beady Eyes — for spotting insects, automobiles

Scaley covering — for protection from the elements during lengthy armadillo races

Nine bands of indestructible armor — for protection from hard blows and Old Blue's teeth

Snout-like nose — designed for rooting in gardens, flower beds

Balloon-like Stomach — Inflates when threatened or faced with long distances to swim

Claw-like feet — for diggin' a 'diller den